by
David Waisglass
and Gordon Coulthart

Andrews and McMeel
A Universal Press Company
Kansas City

ISBN: 0-8362-1704-7
Library of Congress Catalog Card Number: 92-75356

Farcus (fär-kis) 1. *v.* to bungle or botch, to act like an unspeakably mindless dolt, e.g. buying an orchard in the Arctic; 2. *n.* a moronic person inflicted with the intelligence of a dinner mint, e.g. someone who thinks frozen orange juice comes from Arctic orchards; 3. *n.* a futile event, humorous representation of working life, e.g. a non-existent reality, just down the hall and to your left.

WAISGLASS/COULTHART

Bob finally gets the recognition he deserves.

"It keeps our insurance premiums down."

"I don't know ... somehow I thought it would be different."

"We're trying to reduce the paperwork."

6

"I don't understand ... it works on paper."

"Ya, we heard it up here too!"

"... and now I'd like to discuss new ways to fight our absenteeism problem."

"You got 25 years for a system error?"

"Should I hold your calls?"

"He says he likes to work with people."

"... and he's got leadership potential."

"It makes kind of a growling sound."

"Before you go, could you tell me where you put the Kenshaw file?"

"Psst … Harry, does our benefit plan cover this?"

"What d'ya mean, you don't need any more consultants?"

"Send in Furlow. I have some numbers to run by him."

"It's an advertisement for a new courier service."

"We could start by building a railway!"

"I hear there's an opening on the 22nd floor."

"... and without nuclear physics, we wouldn't be here today."

"Can't you file a grievance like everyone else?"

"It's our new telephone system. Notice how long the string is this time."

"Oh look, honey! She drew an organization chart!"

"Harris, you're taking my open door policy a bit too far."

"I wasn't going to ask him to move!"

**What began with a few pencils
and paper clips ...**

"Hey, that looks like one of those letter bombs!"

"Maybe it's time you took a break from Juvenile Court."

"You know, Doc, I like this 'no frills' therapy, but maybe you could buy a couch."

"You're right, we do have enough paper clips."

"Perhaps you should speak to my supervisor."

"$365? Sounds fair to me."

"I'm telling you, every hut has one!"

"Ms. Kelsey, did you get rid of that salesman yet?"

"After all, Freemont ... a deadline is a deadline."

"Hello, photocopy repair?"

vhat exactly did you do at the y Chicken Credit Union?"

"I'm telling ya, honey, any bozo can run this company."

"It's our new computer security system!"

No class travel.

"For $10,000, I can sell you a franchise."

"Think of it as a payroll deduction."

"My prognosis? Thank goodness! I thought it was our sales picture."

"Well, at least you got the job security you wanted."

"We don't have any big ones. But I can give you two small ones for the same price."

"Nonsense ... after 25 years, you deserve it!"

"Oh, umm, we were just going over some files."

"White sugar? Are you nuts? That stuff can kill you."

"Okay, okay. No more Japanese management seminars."

"The crumbs were much bigger before the recession."

"I want an eight percent increase in my allowance and a benefit plan."

"It does multiple graphs and my shorts at the same time."

"... and it runs on remote control!"

"Hey look! I've been invited to a roast!"

"... and then he suggested a career in the public service."

"I know it's tradition, Nick — but you can't discriminate against tall people anymore."

"Your Honor, my client, Flamo the Magnificent, is not a threat to society."

"You're late, Bizley. And that ax murderer excuse won't work this time."

"I think you should forget about this organic shampoo idea."

"Honest, my name *is* Howard Johnson!"

"It's your new image, Nick."

"Okay, so what else does it do?"

"I thought 'good accounting practices' was just a suggestion."

"Okay, okay. But it's my turn next!"

"I should have taken the watch."

"Actually, I'm not your secretary. I'm the Second Assistant for the Apprentice in Training to the Executive's Chief Aide.

24

"I'm telling ya, these are the first signs of inflation."

"What does the flashing red light mean?"

"Excuse me, Your Honor, but I believe I was here first."

"Say, is this in our job description?"

"Good news, Smitsberg! The boss agrees you should have a bigger paycheck."

"Bently, you idiot! I said hire a *paralegal*."

"Henderson, I think you misunderstood our dress code."

"It'll cut down on the number of work breaks!"

WAISGLASS/COULTHART

"Psst. 'Union,' pass it on."

"I told you we'd get a dental plan."

"I hate when they give us junk bonds."

"Do we really need all those channels?"

28

"Can you see the serial number from where you are?"

"That's the third smoker we've lost this week."

"Your 10 o'clock appointment is here."

When stress management works too well.

"And, of course, we have stock options."

"No thanks, it gives me heartburn."

miley. Send in the ducks."

"Careful, guys, I've seen this scam before."

"Your father wonders why you don't play with your club anymore."

"... and transfer this to my account."

"Yeah, they laid off the horses last week."

EMPLOYMENT AGENCY

"This is my stunt double. I won't do anything dangerous."

31

"... so how long did you work at the Mrs. Gooey Cookie Factory?"

"I see your art grant finally came through."

"I'm not sure, but I'd say it's job burn out."

"Mr. Simms is our new quality control supervisor."

"We cut out the middleman."

"Greetings. We seek new markets."

"Do you have other references besides Snake and Butthead?"

"Of course I know the penalty for perjury, but I'd be in more trouble if I told the truth."

"Honey, have you seen the remote control?"

34

"Borman, we've had a few complaints about your recruiting methods."

"Some days I just don't feel good about this job."

"Uh-oh, Harold's getting another fax."

"Tell me things went well in Chicago, Rimstead."

"I understand, but I would hardly call the summer months unconstitutional."

"Maybe this job-sharing plan isn't a good idea."

"Damn it, Smithers. Keep still."

"C'mon guys. We'll never get this done if you don't stop running around."

"This electric car is not one of your better ideas."

Dexter creates the X-91 computer in his own image.

"Frequent flier points. Why do you ask."

"... and he was in charge of employee morale."

"Remember, Gilbert, these corporate retreats build character."

"Hey! How about you be the anchor for a while?"

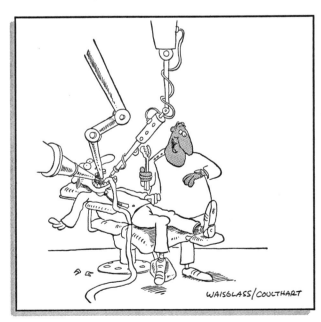

"Say, is it lunch time already?"

"Okay. You've got 15 minutes! What's wrong with me?"

"Good luck, Eddie."

"Okay, okay. I'm a workaholic."

"Wow! This is the biggest iron deposit
I've ever seen."

"... and the guys down the hall
are working on the trap."

Breakfast with an engineer.

"So, you're the new ideas man ..."

"... and then they cut my travel allowance."

"Well, this finalizes your legal separation ..."

"It's our new employee recognition award."

"Well, it may not be art to you!"

Early map-making techniques.

"If you turn it up to 'high,' you can make hot dogs."

"Say, Ed, how long have you been on nights?"

"I'm telling you, people really go for this stuff."

"It seems we have a recruiting officer who can't say *no*."

"Are you programmed to compute the truth, the whole truth ..."

"Okay, now bring it down slowly."

"I don't get it. We've checked every circuit and it still won't boot."

"Let me guess — you've been transferred from Research and Development."

"Say, do you have a real estate agent?"

"They're going back to Personnel."

"Okay, that's good. Now smile ..."

"Nobody takes these security cameras seriously."

"It worked, didn't it?"

"I don't think we need a computer to solve our marital problems."

"Tell me about your first program."

"It looks like we own another savings and loan."

"Say, what kind of bait are you using?"

"Does it come on disk?"

WAISGLASS/COULTHART

Near the end, Lloyd could read the writing on the wall.

"All in favor of shooting that duck …"

"No need to worry, Milrod. We all make mistakes."

48

"It's our soup of the day."

"Gee, things *are* getting tight around here."

"Right here, Section 4A, 'Man's Best Friend'… it doesn't say anything about fetching."

"It's your office. They want to know if you can stay home sick for a few more days."

"My dog ate it."

"Maybe I need a bigger sign."

"I was cleaning it."

"You were the best P.R. man we ever had."

"Say, this isn't 35th and Main."

"Dad says, 'Get a job.' But being a leech is all I know."

"You've got only three weeks to retirement. *You* hit him."

"So, Bob, tell us about our financial picture."

"I'm sorry, Mr. Grimswell, you can't write off your son as a loss."

"We installed some new equipment in your office while you were away."

"You didn't think jumping out of a 10-story building would get rid of me, did you?"

52

"It's an old idea, but damned if it doesn't work."

"There, I think he sees us now."

"Don't ask if they're fresh."

"It's a convenience store."

"... Then it's agreed, this company lacks leadership."

Before fridge magnets.

"Oh, yes! That's definitely you."

"Of course we'll tell you the location of the new office. Just give us a few more days."

54

"Say, haven't I met some of you before?"

"Gentlemen, I propose we buy the Wigworld Toupee Company."

"Does it come in pastel?"

"Hold on, the ball is coming."

"We deducted the army you lost last week."

"Got to work on those power brakes ..."

"... and I'd like to thank everyone who did my job for me."

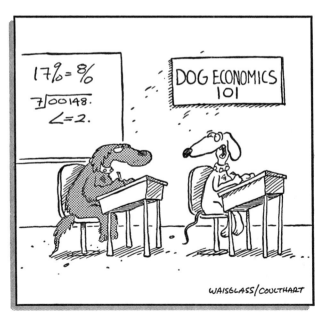

"Remember when all we had to do was fetch?"

"Sorry Grimswhite, this is a smoke-free workplace."

"This package is damaged.
Do I get a discount?"

"I'm not sure, but I think it's a marketing
problem."

"I've seen this before ... Just don't open
the trunk."

"C'mon sister, don't believe everything
you read."

"Bently has been the scapegoat for some of the largest companies in the country."

"Damn mouse!"

"Call me paranoid, but I think people at work are making fun of me."

"Show off!"

"Inventory control, Fran. Can't wait to show you the barn."

"Okay, Babstock, this time you can make the siren noise."

"Because I'm the boss, that's why!"

"You've got a disease I can't pronounce."

60

"Last time I saw Binkman, he was trying to access his computer files."

"Kenshaw, about this brief you sent me…"

"Someone is stealing paper clips on the second floor. Take 'em out."

"I bought it on an installment plan."

61

"Okay, now add a 'pinch of salt' …"

at I sent you to college for?"

"Looks like another slow news day."

"Love the idea, Bingham. But where do we get
the tiny workers?"

"Sometimes I think management has no regard for our welfare."

"Painting is the only time I get to really loosen up."

latest trend in fast food."

"Three more cases and we'll have enough for payroll."

"You can wear Ted's jacket. He won't be here this year."

"Lost that darn watch again."

"Get out of the way, farm boy. We want what's in the silo."

"Say, didn't I vote for you last year?"

"Never hire a lawyer from the help wanted ads."

"We couldn't afford a photographer."

"Forgive me, Father, for I have mismanaged."

"Say, while you're up there, could you hang this for me?"

"And this is the ulcer I got on the Kenshaw account."

"Are you Al?"

"You love your work more than me."

"Seeing you brought a gun, N
why don't you start the meet

"Damn it, Grimwell, you won't get anywhere if you let people treat you like a doormat!"

"... Are you trying to tell me I'm fired?"

"It's a compromise on the health club we wanted."

"Hey, look guys! The company is building us an exercise room."

WAISGLASS/COULTHART

"I remember when a simple water balloon would satisfy you."

"Sorry, I don't deal with people anymore."

"Do you ever wonder what they put in these things?"

"Oh yeah? Well my dad does more insider trading than your dad!"

"Does this come in 8-track?"

"Would you like a gun with that?"

"He can't come to the phone. He's studying for a stress management course."

"Honey. I'm just going to pick up a few things for dinner."

"... and in this one, I keep all our foreign investment."

"Wow! I just jammed the air traffic control tower."

"Wow! I've always wanted an in-ground pool table."

"Relax, everyone. It's just a piece of paper."

REDWOOD   FIREWOOD   DEADWOOD

"You can sit in Hobson's desk. He won't be in today."

"It was easy after I figured out
his access number."

"He wants me to thaw him when
the recession is over."

"Our day-care program offers a better
return on investment."

"Oh yeah? Well my mom's lawyer can
beat up your mom's lawyer!"

"Duffy sure has a way with visual aids."

"I'd love to attend this year's company picnic, but I'm far too wealthy to bother."

"They liked my proposal, but suggested I leave Teddy at home."

"Your insurance only covers our cheapest bypass valves."

"This is Rex. He's been hired through our affirmative action program."

"Maybe the car pool won't be so crowded tomorrow."

"Even though we're shipwrecked with no chance of survival, I'm still your boss!"

"This is our paper cut clinic."

"They still haven't found that missing refrigerator repairman."

"I think you're getting too comfortable in your position here, Smithers."

"Hey, Vinnie, wake up. The boss wants to know if you want to work overtime."

"I can't find a position to suit my lifestyle."

"Look, Mom! I just made all the phones in the house cordless."

"Don't take this personally."

"How's my appeal going?"

"Let me get this straight — the on this committee has decided is to a new committee."

"I was laid off during my job interview."

"Quick! I need 10,000 more temps."

"I'm tellin' ya, honey, I'll never have to buy another suit!"

"My accountant says I'm a rich man trapped in a poor man's body."

"That should do it."

"Why do I always get the tough districts?"

"Congratulations! You finally got your own office."

"Are you kidding? I specialize in negligence!"

82

"Hey, pal, got an opener?"

"… and Consolidated Steel is giving away a free pizza with every 10,000 shares!"

"Once these guys find out where you live, there's no getting rid of them."

"His brother knows the owner."

"This was the only drug rehabilitation center I could afford."

The first practical joke.

"I call it, 'Summer Song.'"

"This time we strike! Last year's slow down was a bust."

"I suggest we sell all our assets and buy lottery tickets."

"... and that's our profit for this quarter, Mr. Morrow."

"They overbook every time I fly."

"You mean you've been locked in this stairway for three years?"

"Here's the history book I borrowed."

"Give me acid rain any day."

"C'mon kid, nobody rolls their own anymore."

WAISGLASS/COULTHART

"Mr. Smithers says you can come back when you say you're sorry."

"Maybe it was the red and black ones I wasn't suppose to cross."

"It was this or a union."

"Bob, could you pick me up after work? Bring your wet suit."

"... and you realize, of course, our insurance premiums will now cost more."

"This microchip is replacing you, Figwood. But if it makes you feel better, it doesn't work either."

"... and just when I was about to give up on this company."

"I remember when you didn't need a college degree."

"Mom, I told you never to call when I'm working."

e have a candidate who can attract a crowd."

"We can't print this, Frank. It's too close to the truth."

"... of course, you know this is going on your permanent record."

"I know you ordered steak, but fish is much better for you."

"On Dasher! On Prancer! Or I'll contract out!

"Excuse me, sir ... You have our pen."

"It says here the air traffic controllers walked off the job this morning."

"Milner, we finally found a job for you that doesn't require any computer training."

"Our file clerk quit in '78"

"You know, carpentry wasn't my first career choice."

"But Mom, you said I should get
a summer job!"

"Don't worry, Bob.
Mr. Flatch respects honesty."

"Wow, how did you know I was looking
for a fortune-teller?"

"Next time you do that, you're fired!"

"Payroll will be ready in a few minutes."

"Sorry about the flambé. … Would you like me to fill your glass while I'm here?"

It wasn't exactly what he expected, but finally Harold's ship came in.

"Does this seem a little too easy?"

"Quick, where's the bathroom?"

The first layoff.

**"Well, this takes care of the job stress
I was having."**

**"Wherever you are, Frank, we knew you'd
want cable."**

"Now Tom, you agree to warm your hands before milking ... and Janet, you promise not to wander."